Making Music

Blowing

Angela Aylmore

Heinemann
LIBRARY

Little Nippers

www.heinemann.co.uk/library
Visit our website to find out more information about **Heinemann Library** books.

To order:
☎ Phone 44 (0) 1865 888066
▤ Send a fax to 44 (0) 1865 314091
▯ Visit the Heinemann Bookshop at www.heinemann.co.uk/library to browse our
catalogue and order online.

First published in Great Britain by Heinemann Library, Halley Court, Jordan Hill, Oxford OX2 8EJ, part of Harcourt Education.
Heinemann is a registered trademark of Harcourt Education Ltd.
© Harcourt Education Ltd 2005.
First published in paperback in 2005.
The moral right of the proprietor has been asserted.

Editorial: Kathy Peltan and Kate Bellamy
Design: Jo Hinton-Malivoire and Bigtop
Picture Research: Ruth Blair
Production: Severine Ribierre

Originated by Chroma Graphics (Overseas) Pte Ltd.
Printed and bound in China by South China Printing Company

ISBN 0 431 08822 5   (hardback)
09 08 07 06 05
10 9 8 7 6 5 4 3 2 1

ISBN 0 431 08827 6   (paperback)
09 08 07 06 05
10 9 8 7 6 5 4 3 2 1

British Library Cataloguing in Publication Data
Aylmore, Angela
Making Music: Blowing
788
A full catalogue record for this book is available from the British Library.

Acknowledgements
The publishers would like to thank the following for permission to reproduce photographs: Alamy pp. **15**, **16**; Corbis pp. **5a**, **13**, **17**, **18**; Getty Images p. **14** (photodisc); Harcourt Education pp. **4a** (Trevor Clifford), **5a**, **5b**, **6**, **7**, **8**, **9**, **10a**, **10b**, **11**, **12**, **19**, **20**, **21**, **22-23** (Tudor Photography).

Cover photograph of a boy playing a trumpet, reproduced with permission of Tudor Photography/Harcourt Education.

Every effort has been made to contact copyright holders of any material reproduced in this book. Any omissions will be rectified in subsequent printings if notice is given to the publishers.

The paper used to print this book comes from sustainable resources.

Contents

Let's make music!

We can make music by blowing!

Nia is playing her recorder.

Blow the harmonica!

Play the recorder

Can you play the recorder?

Blow it gently.
Make a **soft** note.

6

Blow it hard.
Make a
loud note.

Long and short

Play some **short** notes.

peep

peep

peep

peep

Make your own

Can you make an instrument to blow?

Use a bottle and some water.

Blow your bottle.

Make it humm!

11

Sounds like...

Listen to this whistle.
What could it be?

13

High and low

This is a flute.

The flute makes a **soft** high sound

This is a big, tuba!

The tuba makes a **deep** and low sound.

What is it?

This is a shofar.

It comes from Israel.

It is made
from a
ram's horn.

Can you play a horn?

17

Fingers and feet

Fingers that go up and down.
Feet that march around.

Can you make a marching band?

March in time to the music!

19

Listen carefully

What can you hear?

What makes that sound?

recorder

maracas

violin

triangle

It's the recorder!

21

All together now!

whoo whoo

toot toot

Let's all play together!

peep
peep
trr trr

23

Index

Notes for adults

Making Music provides children with an opportunity to think about sound and the different ways instruments can be played to create music. The concept of volume, rhythm, speed and pitch are introduced, and children are encouraged to think about how controlling their movements can create different sounds when they play instruments. The following Early Learning Goals are relevant to this series:

Creative development - music
• explore the different sounds of instruments and learn how sounds can be changed

Knowledge and understanding of the world
• look closely at similarities, differences, patterns and change
• show an interest in why things happen and how things work

Physical development
• respond to rhythm by means of gesture and movement
• manage body to create intended movements

This book looks at different ways of creating music by blowing. It covers different instruments that can be blown and the type of sounds that they make. Children are encouraged to think about how to playing quickly, slowly, loudly and quietly.

Follow-up activities

• Using a recorder, or similar instrument, play two notes to the children. Ask them to identify whether the second note was higher or lower than the first.

• Play the children an example of a piece of music, such as Peter and the Wolf by Sergei Prokofiev. Can they pick out any instruments that you blow from the piece? Can they name them?

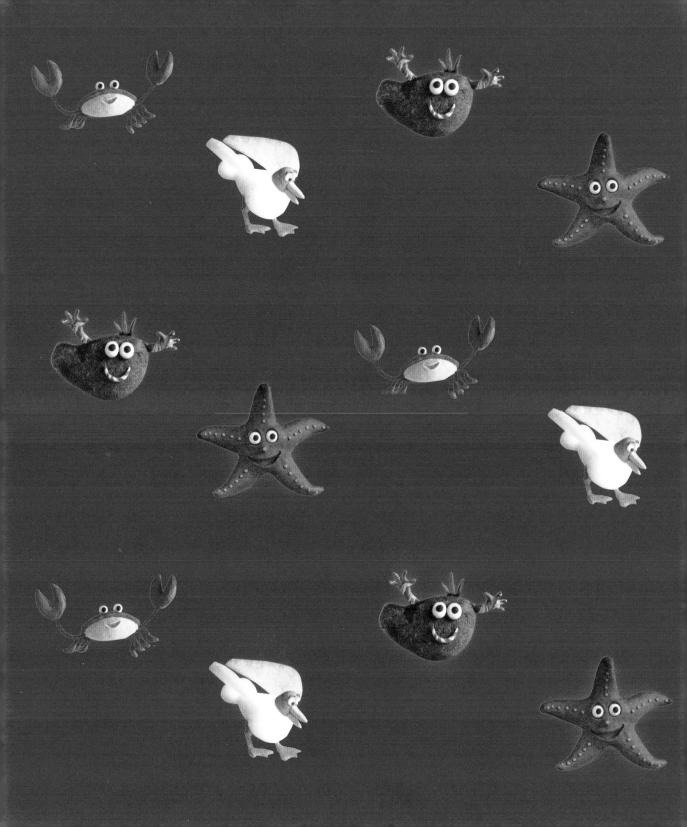